dancing with angels

with angels

Involving survivors in mental health training

by
David Crepaz-Keay, Chris Binns and Evelyn Wilson

CW00822220

introduction

Survivors of mental health services have become increasingly involved in the provision and evaluation of the services they receive and in training and staff development of the professionals who deliver them. They contribute a unique and crucial perspective.

A training event organised by CCETSW London and South East in 1996, attended by trainers, managers and social workers, focused on survivor involvement in the training and continuing professional development of Approved Social Workers (ASWs). Issues discussed included survivor involvement in planning, management, monitoring and evaluation, selection and assessment of candidates, and survivors as training providers.

This guide has been developed from the work of the facilitators and participants at this event but its content is relevant to mental health training in general. Some of the checklists and examples given specifically refer to ASW training but you will find they are just as applicable to the training and staff development of a wide range of mental health professionals.

We also hope the guide will serve as a companion to *The Survivors' Guide to Training Approved Social Workers* published by CCETSW in 1995 which was aimed at the survivors themselves.

Finding your way around the guide

The guide begins with *Getting Started* in a climate of conflicting demands on you as managers and trainers; it identifies some excuses that may hold you back and some responses to move you forward. Ideas for identifying local survivor groups are included.

The focus of Chapter Two is *Sustaining Involvement*. Use of contracts for survivor contributors, clarification of outcomes and setting targets are discussed. Two scenarios, one of a new survivor group and the other about choosing a Black survivor trainer, illustrate ways to facilitate the development of good survivor contributors.

Chapter Three *Evaluation* considers ways to check out that survivor involvement is working from the survivor's perspective and discusses the importance of giving feedback to survivor trainers and suggestions on how to go about it.

The idea for the illustrations came from a sculpt in one of the small groups at the training event. The poem and stories that form two of the *Interludes* have been provided by two survivors and demonstrate the power of poetry and story telling as a way of conveying personal perspectives and experiences. The third *Interlude* takes a trainer's perspective on involving survivors.

Whatever stage you are at in involving survivors there is room for improvement both for the survivors and for the programme providers and you are encouraged to make your own action plan. The Guide finishes with a *Checklist* for involving survivors.

Expectations and hopes

We hope that this guide will encourage you to:

- push back the limits on using survivor trainers
- increase confidence in involving survivors
- avoid tokenism
- involve Black survivor trainers and contributors
- reflect and prepare for involving survivors
- broaden knowledge of survivor groups and trainers
- deal with resistance to survivor involvement
- improve practice and see the positive effects on service delivery of involving survivors.

Involving survivors in mental health training and staff development is, in our view, a necessary and enriching process. We hope you will share these expectations and be encouraged and supported by the guide in involving survivors.

Note on words and meanings: The term 'survivor' is most frequently used throughout this guide to describe those people who have been through the psychiatric system and survived. Survivors are self defined and choose the term to reflect a positive approach to their experience. The term is not universal and 'user' and 'service user' are also found in the guide. Other self definitions include 'ex-user', 'consumer' and 'recipient'. Each has its merits and so long as people are defining themselves, there is little more to be said.

getting started

Decision making

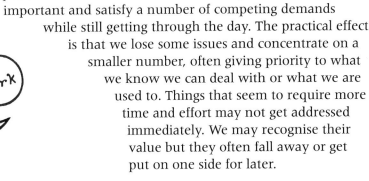

In our everyday lives we have a myriad of decisions to make. We have to prioritise what is important and satisfy a number of competing demands while still getting through the day. The practical effect is that we lose some issues and concentrate on a smaller number, often giving priority to what we know we can deal with or what we are used to. Things that seem to require more time and effort may not get addressed immediately. We may recognise their value but they often fall away or get put on one side for later.

Most of us will agree that the idea of involving survivors in mental health training and staff development is a good thing. But getting started may well take additional time, effort, money and commitment.

We need to look at how meeting competing demands, priority setting and decision-making impacts on the way survivors are involved in mental health training and staff development. Being on the end of decisions made for us may induce feelings of:

lack of ownership
being underestimated
marginalisation
frustration
powerlessness
self doubt
anger.

In contrast, decisions in which we have participated will induce feelings of:

ownership
involvement
self respect
acceptance
expertise
equality.

The message coming out of this list is that in order to involve survivors well they need to be involved at the planning stage of your programme. Excuses, however, may still be made for delay in involving them.

Excuse busters

What hinders progress in involving survivors? Below are some common excuses or blocks to survivor involvement with some suggested excuse busters. Many of the excuses and responses are interchangeable.

Subject	Excuse	Excuse buster
Survivors as trainers	They're not ready for it	The only way people can become experienced trainers is by training. A good way to help people into training is by encouraging them on to courses as participants. Also consider asking experienced trainers to co-train.
	They are not representative/ not like our clients	Sometimes you just can't win. As soon as you overcome the lack of experience, you are no longer a typical user! Most trainers of any profession are not typical simply because most professionals, just like most survivors, aren't trainers. Acquiring and using training skills empowers people in a way that mental health services don't – but you don't lose your understanding of distress, or of the best/worst of services by becoming a trainer. You just get better at passing them on.

Survivors as trainers (continued)	We haven't got a budget for it	This doesn't stop people getting other trainers.
	The effect on benefits	Just as professionals receive payment for their work, survivors should be similarly remunerated. Direct payments will have an effect on those on benefits. However, there are ways in which payments can be made without affecting benefits e.g. making fees payable to a user group account; encouraging and supporting survivor trainers in setting up a consortium; and paying fees through weekly payments at therapeutic earnings level.
Survivors in programme planning, management and monitoring	There's too much asked of too few survivors	Consider pairing survivors with a more experienced survivor contributor to the programme in order to share the development of confidence and skills.
	They're not ready for it	Remember that many people, including survivors, don't like committees. There are other ways in which people can be involved.
Survivors in selection and assessment (where applicable)	Confidentiality	Like so many objections to survivor involvement this one assumes that they are somehow less reliable than professionals. The answer is to agree clear ground rules about the process with all involved.

Staff prejudice	Sadly, this is often at the root of all blocks to and excuses used to avoid involving survivors in anything. Acknowledging it is at least half the battle. Addressing prejudice is definitely a training issue. Going ahead with training often works as a way of proving the prejudices to be wrong.
They don't understand the criteria/equal opportunities reasons	Selection criteria and equal opportunities approaches are not beyond comprehension to all but the most highly skilled professionals! However, it seems sometimes as though explaining them in simple terms is beyond the people making the excuse. This is their failing not the survivors'.
There isn't time to involve them properly	The sooner you introduce survivors to any process, the more satisfactory will be the outcome. Involving people at a late stage is less than ideal, and can smack of tokenism. However, involving survivors at the current stage of a process will give them some experience and understanding that will help them to be more effectively involved next time round.

Survivors in practice development and project work	They won't understand what's expected	See "They don't understand the criteria".
	People in crisis couldn't cope with the work	It is unreasonable to suggest that gaining survivor feedback on the performance for example of an ASW during a Mental Health Act assessment becomes part of the assessment process. This does not, however, prevent follow up with the survivor at a later date. People are not always in crisis.
	The system won't allow it	Generally this is not the case. If it is, change the system.
	Confidentiality (again)	aaaarrrggghhh!!!!
	Conflict of interest between service users and the staff with whom they are involved	People can feel inhibited about making negative comments about professionals on whom they rely for a service. The responsibility for creating a mechanism that feels safe lies with the professionals.

Black survivors as trainers	We don't know any – they are hard to find	You've got to start somewhere. Try approaching a local Black community group. A genuine request for help will induce a positive response. "This is what we want. How can you help us?"
	Not the 'right sort' of Black survivor	Who says? – the Black community, your boss, you?
	Not relevant, no Black people here	Working with difference and understanding the Black perspective is essential to all mental health professionals. Don't assume that there are no Black people in your community or that all programme participants are White.
	It might subject them to racism or stereotyping	Agree clear ground rules for participants and contributors.

Offer Black survivors support in how to present their material. Consider the issues that may arise and how they might deal with them.

Consider using two or three Black survivors in an all-White environment, or offer to go out to their territory. |

| **Black survivors as trainers** (continued) | Our local group doesn't have any Black survivors | Some survivor groups have difficulty in involving Black survivors. You need to nudge them towards grappling with Black issues. How about setting survivor groups a target in their contract for increasing the number of Black members? Or you could fund a Black survivor development worker for 12 months to develop resources in a survivor group.

If you are in a part of the UK where there are few Black survivors, educate yourself by going to where there is more experience and bring what you learn back to your community. |
| | The Black survivor we use is getting burnt out | Black survivor trainers are often over used. Support your community to develop more people with skills as above. |
| | They don't speak English in the local Asian women's mental health group | They have just as much if not more experience that we need to hear about. But it will take more preparation and planning. Make use of local link workers and interpreting services. Course participants can learn from the process and transfer the good use of interpreters and link workers to their work with survivors. |

| Black survivors don't want to get involved | Black survivors may be reluctant to be involved. Mental health training cannot be divorced from the alienation Black communities feel from White institutions. Involvement in training may be seen as placing oneself in a vulnerable position – having had little control over the way other services are delivered, why should this be different? |

"We're not mad, we're angry!"

"White people will never understand how we feel."

Many survivors dislike being asked about their personal experiences. You need to recognise this as reality and be proactive.

An excuse is the skin of a reason stuffed with the sausage of a lie.

Identifying local resources

Many areas have local survivor or service user groups already, often without the knowledge of statutory services. Quite a number of such groups exist for a specific group of people – Asian women, or young people, for example. Access to these may be found through local directories of community organisations or mental health associations. Some of these groups will be a useful source of specialist trainers – but remember an Asian woman trainer should not be expected to do just the Asian Women and Mental Health slot!

Below is a list of national organisations that should be able to put you in touch with any local groups of which they are aware:

African and Caribbean Users and Survivors Forum
c/o Lambeth Mental Health Centre, 332 Brixton Road, London SW9 7AA
Tel: 0171 738 6667

Hearing Voices Network
c/o Creative Support, Dale House, 35 Dale Street, Manchester M1 2HF
Tel and Fax: 0161 228 3896

MINDLINK
15-19 Broadway, Stratford, London E15 4BQ
Tel: 0181 519 2122 Fax: 0181 522 1725

Scottish Users Network
18/19 Claremont Crescent, Edinburgh EH7 4QD
Tel: 0131 557 4969 Fax: 0131 556 0279

Survivors Speak Out
34 Osnaburgh Street, London NW1 3ND
Tel: 0171 916 5472 Fax: 0171 916 5473

The United Kingdom Advocacy Network [UKAN]
Volserve House, 14-18 West Bar Green, Sheffield S1 2DA
Tel, Fax and Minicom: 0114 272 8171

US The All Wales User Network
Office Suite 3, 1 North Parade, Aberystwyth SY23 2JH
Tel: 01970 626230 Fax: 01970 626233

Interlude I

Leckcha

Dacta, tell me sumtin
A wen yu du all yu studyin
An readin an tings

Dem nevah tell yu
Bout
Umanity, campasshan
Sympatty, sensitivitty

Well, let me tell yu sumtin
Yu si dis sad ol man
Im famly foun dead in di back of a van
Im granson crush anda di wheels of a tram
Noh bodda caall it "depresshan"
Is a ting caal life
Di uman candishan

Yu doan ear bout it yet?

Yu doan see how
Di puleece dem
Beat up on di yout dem
How anga fly up inna evahone face
No boddah caal it "psychosis"
Is a fac of life
Di uman candishan

Yu doan know it yet?

Yu si dis ooman
Stealin a lickle food and drink
Fi er children dem
Well di courts caal it "illegal"
Di dacta caal it "schizophrenia"
Evahbaddy else caal it "survival"
Is a ting caal life
De uman candishan

Dacta, tell me sumtin
A wen yu du all yu studyin
An readin an tings

Dem nevah tell yu
Bout
Question evahtin yu read
An question evahtin dem seh
Dem nevah tell yu
Bout
Camman sense
Did dey?

Quibilah Montsho © 1996

16

sustaining involvement

Benefits of involvement

One of the best ways to maintain meaningful involvement of survivors is for the benefits of their involvement to be clearly seen. Start by looking at why you want to involve survivors and what the people you wish to involve expect to come out of the process.

Everyone will have their own reasons. The checklist that follows is drawn from an ASW programme. It is not exhaustive and you are encouraged to add to it.

Outcomes checklist
✔ ensure a survivor interest/perspective permeates all aspects of the programme planning and management
✔ explore survivor movement models of understanding mental distress
✔ increase understanding of common experiences of survivors of services
✔ support the development of practice skills that maximise the respect, dignity and power of recipients of Mental Health Act assessments and social work services
✔ consider issues of risk, hazard and danger from survivors' perspectives
✔ consider the place of independent advocacy and the use of compulsion from a survivor movement perspective

✔ explore the role of the ASW as a developer of survivor-led services and gain survivor perspectives on local services

✔ establish partnership models in relation to future service and practice development.

Clearly thinking through and noting expected outcomes leads naturally into other parts of this guide. Outcomes can form the basis of contracts (see below) and make the process of feedback and evaluation (chapter three) much easier and more objective. They can also help less experienced survivor groups or trainers prepare more effectively for their contribution and, when combined with effective feedback and evaluation, will support their development.

> **Important note:** *when you start to engage survivors in training and staff development, be aware that what may be clear and unambiguous to you may sound like jargon to others. Simply giving a survivor group a copy of the formal training requirements is neither effective communication nor a clear statement of desired outcomes, so is unlikely to lead to good well-focused training by survivor trainers.*

Use of contracts/agreements

A contract is not only a requirement of many social services departments who purchase a service, it also offers a way of formalising what is expected of both the professional(s) and the survivor(s) involved. While all concerned will need to bear in mind any constraints on some survivors who receive benefits (see *Excuse Busters* page 8), for freelance survivor consultants contracts generally make things a lot easier.

Target setting

Sustaining involvement will also be supported by setting and monitoring specific targets for survivor involvement in your training programme. For example:

● two survivors on the programme planning and review board in the next 12 months
● survivor trainer input into risk management training programme in the next nine months.

Facilitating the development of good survivor contributors

The following two scenarios illustrate ways to facilitate the development of survivor contributors.

(1) *Scenario One:* **Involving a survivor group**
Your ASW training has always used one or two well known survivor trainers. A fledgling survivor group has just formed locally and you are keen to involve them.

What happens next?

Things to consider
● What do you want to involve people in?
● What do the group want to offer?
● What is needed to develop the group and the training programme?
● Who defines outcomes?
● Who teaches what?

Comments

This situation will be familiar to some. In a number of areas around the UK, established survivor trainers have encouraged staff to promote the setting up of local survivor groups. In other places, survivor trainers have been asked to facilitate their development. In either case resistance from survivor trainers is unlikely, unless they believe the new group is being set up to fail. There are a number of approaches that have worked well in this situation – leading to broader survivor training and better development of the local group.

The perspectives offered by experienced survivor trainers are likely to be different from those of a newly established group. The new group should, in the first instance, be considered as an additional resource. They will be more aware of local problems and appropriate responses. A local group is more likely to be familiar with a range of local resources that will not be known to either social services, or someone from a national survivor organisation.

Local group members should be offered, when practical, the opportunity to sit in on training programmes as participants. One advantage is that they will become more aware of the roles and responsibilities of the professionals; they will also increase their understanding of the legislation involved. Perhaps of equal importance, as course participants, they will get to see a range of different trainers, and training techniques in action. The would-be trainers will then have a pool of ideas on which to draw for later use.

Experienced survivor trainers will be able to complement this with examples of new ideas from around the UK. Nearly every area in which survivors train will have something different to offer people using their services. The best of these can be explored by those who travel and train widely, and the lessons learned can then be passed around. Similarly, when it comes to planning and monitoring courses, experience of a range of approaches can bring an additional dimension to the process. This would fit well with good grass roots experience from a local group member on a planning team.

Sitting alongside an old hand is an excellent way for survivors to gain training experience and build confidence. Co-training has become one of the primary methods for introducing new trainers in a relatively safe training situation (it also makes experienced trainers think more carefully about what they do and why when co-trainers ask probing questions of them!).

Support for the fledgling survivor/user group
● Spend time with them
● Offer resources such as training for survivor trainers
● Help them to identify and develop skills
● Give constructive feedback and criticism
● Negotiate outcomes from trainer and survivor perspective.

(2) ### Scenario Two: choosing a Black survivor trainer
When organising a training programme, you identify the need for Black survivor input at planning and monitoring stages and the need to deliver modules of the taught course.

You are given two alternatives:

(1) An articulate angry Black survivor activist, highly regarded by Black survivors who has legitimacy in the Black community. Mental health professionals could regard her as confrontational and separatist. Involving her in any training is asking for trouble.
(2) The active mainly White user group know of a Black survivor who has extensive training experience. However, many Black survivors regard him as on the edge of their community.

He does not involve himself in community activity nor does he relate to other Black survivors very well. They see the user group as a "White people's thing".

Things to consider in making your decision
- your reasons for wanting Black survivor input
- what the two alternative contributors want to offer
- resources or training available for either alternative
- implications of your choice for your relationship with the Black community
- how you will work with this.

Comments
- Clarify the outcomes you seek and any reservations you have with the individuals involved and listen to their response.
- Remember you are contracting with a survivor trainer to provide a service.
- Be aware that the choice you make will be seen as a political decision.
- Use the opportunity to explore unconventional and creative ways of working with survivors.
- Either choice presents an opportunity for dialogue with the survivor group/community about the reason for your decision. This may open up more opportunities to develop survivor involvement in training.
- Put aside time for adequate discussion with and preparation of survivor contributors.
- In briefing Survivor (1) help her to design the session so that she can effectively get her message across and not inhibit learning. Find ways to help her channel her energy constructively.
- Consider different ways of involving her, for example by contributing to practice skills or through poetry or telling stories (see *Interludes I* and *II*).
- Remember that building confidence is an issue for some Black survivors.
- Consider the use of a mentor or pairing with another Black survivor.

Interlude II

Interactive survivor story time

The cloud

Once-upon-a-time, in a small village in the Chilterns, lived a man who could see and hear things other people couldn't. One day, he became aware of a small cloud – it was an evil cloud. Sometimes it would rumble, sometimes it would roar, sometimes it would smell terrible. When the man saw the cloud out of the corner of his eye it would make him jump out of his skin. It kept coming.

Then one wet and windy night, it started to chase him. The man started to run.

(There are two possible endings to this story – the reader can choose what happens next)

Ending A

While the man was running, he was seen by a couple of policemen. They saw him, but they couldn't see the cloud. They tried to talk to him but he just ran. So they ran after him. He was now being chased by policemen as well as the cloud.

Eventually they caught him. He struggled as much as he could, but he was taken under Section 136, and later admitted to hospital. When he finally went home, the cloud was waiting for him...

Ending B

After many miles, the man came to rest. He had outrun the cloud, but he was tired and wet, and cold. He found a telephone box and rang a friend. She came to him and went back with him to his home. The cloud was gone but all the paper had been torn from the wall around the window. The rain was coming through the wall. They found someone to mend the window, got married and lived happily ever after.

Dancing with angels

There was a woman who saw and heard angels. She danced with them and sang with them; they were her friends. No one else ever saw them. At times she was a little difficult to be with, but no worse than that. She was diagnosed as schizophrenic and given Largactil.

She thought the Largactil was killing her angels and refused to take the medication. The pressure to take the medication caused her increasing friction and distress, and she was sectioned. She chose to take her own life rather than live without her angels.

The moral of the stories

Mental health is about finding better ways of dealing with the cloud and with the angels.

evaluation

This chapter covers two important elements in the process of evaluating the involvement of survivor trainers – (1) feedback from programme organisers and trainees to survivors on their contribution to the programme and (2) feedback from survivors on whether survivor involvement is working.

(1) Feedback to survivor trainers

On some mental health training programmes survivors have been involved, as trainers, monitors, or participants, for quite some time. On others, the process has hardly begun. But no matter what stage people are at, there is plenty of room for improvement for both survivors and people running the courses. Feedback, like any form of communication, is a two-way process, so everyone – organisers, trainees and survivors alike – must be prepared to learn from it. And it is an essential part of any improvement. It follows directly from setting outcomes and is the best way to ensure that outcomes are met and continue to be met.

Checklist on feedback

To enable everyone to get the most out of the process, there are a number of things that are particularly important for course organisers and trainees to bear in mind when giving feedback to survivor trainers.

● *Be honest, open and show respect for individual opinion*
There is no point in giving feedback if it is dishonest or incomplete but it should also respect an individual and their point of view. If you have been clear about outcomes, then feedback can be more objective than "that seemed to go all right".

● *Critically appraise survivors' intervention*
How did the session/day/course change as a result of the involvement?
How could the involvement have been (even) more effective?

● *Be reflective and constructive and recognise that feedback is a two-way process*
Whether things go well or badly depends on a wide range of factors of which the survivor's input is just one, albeit a vital one. Any trainer will be well placed to analyse the good and bad bits that were beyond their control, but which may be either repeated or avoided in future.

● *Focus on both strengths and areas for improvement*
Even the worst of training sessions has elements of some merit. Likewise, the best of sessions is unlikely to be perfect. A trainer who has endured a ghastly afternoon will welcome some emphasis on the silver lining. And there is no better time to make those small improvements than when basking in the warm glow of a successful day's work.

● *Don't just write off things that didn't work – examine them*
Both trainer and course co-ordinator should understand why something failed. Possible reasons include:

– the wrong exercise at the wrong time of day;
– a session being out of context with the course;
– trainee fatigue;
– inappropriate venue;
– trying to cover too much ground in too little time.

- ***Provide ongoing feedback***
  This is particularly important for newish local groups. Group development can be greatly enhanced by continued contact.
- ***Check when survivors want feedback***
  Some people would rather get feedback a few days after the training, others like some feedback over a drink immediately after the session. A few people prefer feedback at intervals throughout a session (though this is more likely to be reassurance than feedback proper). If you promise to give someone feedback at a later date, *remember to do so.*
- ***Build principles of giving feedback into the ground rules for training***
  A course co-ordinator may find it useful to make a formal channel for trainee to trainer feedback as part of the ground rules for training. Participants will need to appreciate that challenging professional sacred cows is not a personal insult, rather a different perception of roles.
- ***Be constructive***
  There is little point in giving feedback if things are not going to improve as a result.
- ***Use appropriate and non-threatening language***
  The feedback process should encourage dialogue. Using ill-thought-out language is likely to prompt a defensive response to criticism rather than improvement.
- ***Ground your feedback in sound evidence***
  Inform trainers of the evaluation process and results from internal evaluation where appropriate. Criticism backed with evidence is more likely to lead to improvement and will reduce the risk of a negative reaction.
- ***If someone is simply not likely to be a trainer, let them know why***
  Training is not for everyone. There are many other ways of getting involved. Let people know what these are, and how to pursue them. For example, some programmes require trainees to interview survivors for their perspectives as part of their project work and/or assessed tasks.

> **Note:** *The previous checklist is designed to make feedback more constructive for survivors but most, if not all, of it would improve feedback to any trainers. Like so many areas of survivor involvement improved practice benefits us all.*

(2) Is survivor involvement working?

We have stressed throughout the guide the importance of the agreed outcomes to be expected from involving survivors. These outcomes also form the basis for your judgement of whether survivor involvement is working. Answers from survivors to the following questions may be drawn on when making this judgement.

Some questions for survivors
- Are you being listened to and understood?
- Are your views taken into account in the planning of the provision?
- Are you treated sensitively and respectfully in contributing to learning and assessment?
- Is your feedback included in the mechanisms for evaluating and further developing learning and assessment?
- Have you received constructive feedback from the programme on your contribution?
- What worked well in your contribution?
- Have your outcomes been met?
- Has anything changed as a result?
- What more can we do to support your input to the programme?
- What needs to be done differently?
- Do you want to be involved in the planning and input of the next training programme?

Interlude III

A trainer's tale

Involving survivors is about sharing power.

Sitting down with an experienced survivor trainer to discuss and plan together his input into a 60-day ASW programme meant giving up some things I liked doing.

I was committed to survivor involvement in training and regularly used local and national people to contribute to sessions I had planned for them. I had invited George to meet me in a consultant capacity and welcomed his expertise. We agreed a number of outcomes and an allocation of sessions to meet them. Areas to be included covered survivor movement perspectives on a range of relevant issues.

We also agreed a day to focus practice skills on maximising the dignity of the person being assessed.

An experienced ASW before coming to training, I especially valued facilitating practice skills sessions and thought I did it well.

While hosting the day, I again recognised that George brought a sharpness of perspective to participants in role play on "interviewing in a suitable manner", that offered a more sensitive approach to the person being assessed than brought by me. His authenticity made a crucial impact on participants.

Involving survivors is about recognising their expertise and experience.

checklist and action plans

Possible action plans

As an encouragement for you to move forward, here are some of the next steps proposed by participants in the CCETSW workshop at the end of the two days training.

- *"Tell my manager"*
  If your manager is kept informed and understands the benefits, progress will be much easier to sustain.
- *"Seek more resources"*
  There may be cost implications for involving people. If there are additional sources of funding, the process will be much easier.
- *"Use CCETSW requirements on user orientation in* **Assuring Quality for Mental Health Social Work***"*
- *"Give feedback to my ASW programme management/training steering group"*
  Many training co-ordinators have such groups that can play a vital role in ensuring involvement becomes part of the culture. These groups should be encouraged to involve survivors in their own activities. Involvement should include practice development.
- *"Seek feedback from people who I have assessed at a later date as a regular part of survivor feedback"*

This is absolutely vital if we are to develop survivor-sensitive practice.

● *"Make more time for the process of survivor involvement"*
Involving survivors may be time consuming at first, particularly if starting from scratch. A conscious effort should be made to make time for this process. Allow more time to contact newer survivor groups, or individuals who want to get involved.

End piece

Whatever your role in mental health training and staff development, involving survivors effectively will help you to balance better the other competing demands and give you a larger repertoire of resources.

Involving survivors: a checklist for programme organisers

Have you addressed the following?

✔ Has funding been established before planning begins?
✔ Are survivors involved in:
  – planning the programme
  – delivering learning and assessment
  – monitoring and evaluation?
✔ Have excuses hindering development been addressed?
✔ Have targets with time-scales been set for survivor involvement in the programme?
✔ Have local and national survivor resources/groups been identified?
✔ Have equal opportunities issues, including race and gender, been considered in the choice of people/groups and contributions?
✔ Is difference valued?
✔ Have you clarified the outcomes you expect from involving survivors?
✔ Have training outcomes been agreed with survivor contributors, and written into contracts (where appropriate)?
✔ Have sufficient time and resources been allowed for preparing people/groups?
✔ Are venues, timetables and materials accessible?
✔ Have procedures been established to ensure people are treated sensitively and respectfully?
✔ When and how will you give feedback to people/groups?
✔ When and how will you check out that survivor involvement is working from their perspective?
✔ Is there an action plan for developing survivor involvement?